# THE
## CHURCHILL
### WIT

# THE
# CHURCHILL
# WIT

*Edited by* **BILL ADLER**

**Coward-McCann, Inc.**    **New York**

*By* BILL ADLER

THE KENNEDY WIT

DEAR PRESIDENT JOHNSON

*Library of Congress Catalog Card Number: 65-18290*

PRINTED IN THE UNITED STATES OF AMERICA

PHOTOGRAPHS COURTESY KEYSTONE PRESS
AGENCY, UNITED PRESS INTERNATIONAL, WIDE
WORLD PHOTOS, LONDON DAILY EXPRESS

# *Contents*

# THE
## CHURCHILL
### WIT

# The
# *Churchill*
# *Wit*

This book records the remarkable wit of Winston Spencer Churchill.

During a lifetime that spanned ninety years, Sir Winston Churchill played many roles. He was a statesman, soldier, politician, artist, writer, leader of men and nations. More than any other, he was *the* man of the twentieth century.

Few will forget his rallying trademark in World War II, the reassuring smile and the upraised hand signaling "V" for Victory. Generations yet unborn will marvel at his brilliant command of the English language. As John Fitzgerald Kennedy once said, "Churchill mobilized the English language and sent it into battle."

But this man who led his people through so much turbulent history never lost that unique gift which was his, the ability to lighten a heavy load of responsibility with wit and humor.

Wit abounded in all he wrote and said, on the floor of the House of Commons, in debate with friends and foes, at home, in America, in peace and in war. The brilliance of his humor mirrored the genius of the man.

No man gave more to the twentieth century than Winston Spencer Churchill. We will remember him for much, not least of which was the Churchill wit.

BILL ADLER

*New York City*
*February, 1965*

# POLITICS

## Politics

*Pleading for preparedness in April, 1938, Mr. Churchill wrote:*

We have never been likely to get into trouble by having an extra thousand or two of up-to-date airplanes at our disposal.

As the man whose mother-in-law had died in Brazil replied when asked how the remains should be disposed of:

"Embalm, cremate and bury. Take no chances."

When Churchill was a young man, he was asked to take to a dinner a young lady who had political views which were in direct opposition to Churchill. As a debonair man-about-town, Churchill had just grown a mustache. As they were departing for the dinner, the young lady said, "Mr. Churchill, I care for neither your politics nor your mustache."

"Don't distress yourself," Churchill replied. "You are not likely to come in contact with either."

3

*Question:* Would you tell our readers, sir, what are the
desirable qualifications for any young man who wishes
to become a politician?

*Mr. Churchill:* It is the ability to foretell what is going to
happen tomorrow, next week, next month, and next
year. And to have the ability afterwards to explain
why it didn't happen.

The dignity of a Prime Minister, like a lady's virtue,
was not susceptible of partial diminution.

HOUSE OF COMMONS
*July, 1905*

*Mr. Churchill was offered by the King the Order of the
Garter shortly after his 1945 defeat. He turned it down,
commenting:*

Why should I accept the Order of the Garter from His
Majesty, when the people have just given me the order
of the boot?

The word "disinflation" has been coined in order to
avoid the unpopular term "deflation." I suppose that
presently when "disinflation" also wins its bad name, the
Chancellor [Sir Stafford Cripps] will call it "non-disinfla-
tion," and will start again.

HOUSE OF COMMONS
*October, 1949*

One night in the House of Commons, a Miss Bessie Braddock, a Socialist member for Liverpool, turned to Churchill and said, "Winston, you're drunk." Churchill instantly replied: "Bessie, you're ugly and tomorrow morning I'll be sober but you'll still be ugly."

I hope you have all mastered the official Socialist jargon, which our masters, as they call themselves, wish us to learn.

You must not use the word poor, they are described as the "lower income group."

When it comes to a question of freezing a workman's wages, the Chancellor of the Exchequer speaks of "arresting increases in personal income." The idea is that formerly income tax payers used to be well-to-do and that, therefore, it will be popular and safe to hit at them. Sir Stafford Cripps does not like to mention the word "wages" but that is what he means.

There is a lovely one about houses and homes. They are in the future to be called "accommodation units." I don't know how we are to sing our old song "Home Sweet Home." "Accommodation Unit, Sweet Accommodation Unit, there's no place like our Accommodation Unit."

*Cardiff, February, 1950*

Politics are almost as exciting as war, and quite as dangerous. In war, you can only be killed once, but in politics many times.

*1920*

*When Churchill learned that the Minister of Food was about to establish "communal feeding stations," he wrote a protest to the Minister.*

It is an odious expression suggestive of Communism and the workhouse. I suggest you call them "British restaurants." Everybody associates the word "restaurant" with a good meal, and they might as well have the name if they cannot get anything else.

*Churchill on fanatics:*

A fanatic is one who can't change his mind and won't change the subject.

*Winston Churchill was never fond of Ramsay MacDonald, and in a speech in the House of Commons in 1931, had this to say about him:*

I remember when I was a child being taken to the celebrated Barnum's Circus, which contained an exhibition of freaks and monstrosities, but the exhibit on the program which I desired to see was the one described as "The Boneless Wonder."

My parents judged that spectacle would be too revolting and demoralizing for my youthful eyes, and I have waited fifty years to see "The Boneless Wonder" sitting on the Treasury Bench.

*When MacDonald became Prime Minister, Churchill observed:*

We know that he has, more than any other man, the gift of compressing the largest amount of words into the smallest amount of thought.

*Mr. Churchill was once asked in the House of Commons about the importance of consultation with his political allies and foes. This was his reply:*

Well, one can always consult a man and ask him, "Would you like your head cut off tomorrow?" and after he has said, "I would rather not," cut it off.

*May, 1947*

*A new member of the House of Commons was making a long speech—longer than Churchill thought necessary. After he had finished, Mr. Churchill commented:*

I can understand the honorable member speaking for practice, which he sorely needs.

When I am abroad, I always make it a rule never to criticize or attack the government of my own country. I make up for lost time when I come home.

House of Commons
*April, 1947*

*When the Labour Party (Socialists) took over power from Winston Churchill in 1945, one of their first decisions was to substitute nickel for silver coinage. In a speech in Blackpool, England, Mr. Churchill made this comment:*

And now the British housewife, as she stands in the queues to buy her bread ration, will fumble in her pocket in vain for a silver sixpence. Under the Socialist Government, nickel will have to be good enough for her. In future, we shall still be able to say "every cloud has a nickel lining."

*October, 1946*

I like the martial and commanding air with which the right honorable gentleman treats facts. He stands no nonsense from them.

HOUSE OF COMMONS
*February, 1909*

*Replying to a political opponent in the House of Commons, a young Winston Churchill quipped:*

If I valued the honorable gentleman's opinion, I might get angry.

*January, 1913*

In those days, Mr. Baldwin was wiser than he is now, he used to frequently take my advice.

*May, 1935*

*When Hugh Gaitskell was Labour Party Minister of Fuel and Power in 1947, he campaigned to have fewer baths as a way of saving coal. "I have never had a great many baths myself," he said in a speech, "and I can assure those who have them as a habit that it does not make much difference to their health if they have fewer." Mr. Churchill was not about to let this suggestion by Mr. Gaitskell go without comment:*

When Ministers of the Crown speak like this on behalf of His Majesty's Government, the Prime Minister and his friends have no need to wonder why they are getting increasingly into bad odor.

I have even asked myself whether you, Mr. Speaker, would admit the word lousy as a Parliamentary expression in referring to the Administration, provided, of course, it was not intended in a contemptuous sense but purely as one of factual narration.

HOUSE OF COMMONS
*October, 1947*

*During the postwar Labour Government, Mr. Churchill talked scathingly of Health Minister Aneurin Bevan, whom he called Britain's "Minister of Disease":*

I have no doubt that the highest exponents in the medical profession would concur that a period of prolonged seclusion and relief from any responsible duties would be an equal benefit to Mr. Bevan and to the National Health Service.

*July, 1948*

*Churchill on extremists:*

They make the infinite complexities of scientific civilization and the multitudinous phenomena of great cities conform to a few barbarous formulas which any moderately intelligent parrot could repeat in a fortnight.

*In 1904, Winston Churchill remarked about the then Prime Minister Joseph Chamberlain:*

Mr. Chamberlain loves the working man, he loves to see him work.

*In 1914, Winston Churchill was First Lord of the Admiralty. He had many critics at the time. Of Lord Charles Beresford, one of his chief critics, Churchill said:*

He can best be described as one of those orators who, before they get up, do not know what they are going to say; when they are speaking, do not know what they are saying; and, when they have sat down, do not know what they have said.

*In 1937, Winston Churchill made the following evaluation of the Chamberlain government:*

They are decided only to be undecided, resolved to be irresolute, adamant for drift, all-powerful for impotency.

I must say that this class of criticism which I read in the newspapers when I arrived on Sunday morning reminds me of the simple tale about the sailor who jumped into a dock, I think it was at Plymouth, to rescue a small boy from drowning.

About a week later, this sailor was accosted by a woman who asked, "Are you the man who picked my son out of the dock the other night?"

The sailor replied modestly, "That is true, ma'am."

"Ah," said the woman, "you are the man I am looking for. Where is his cap?"

Many forms of government have been tried and will be tried in this world of sin and woe. No one pretends that Democracy is perfect or all-wise.

Indeed, it has been said that Democracy is the worst form of government except all those other forms that have been tried from time to time.

HOUSE OF COMMONS
*November, 1947*

Lenin was sent into Russia by the Germans in the same way that you might send a phial containing a culture of typhoid or cholera to be poured into the water supply of a great city.

HOUSE OF COMMONS
*November, 1919*

There are two ways in which a gigantic debt may be spread over new decades and future generations. There is the right and healthy way and there is the wrong and morbid way. The wrong way is to fail to make the utmost provision for amortization which prudence allows, to aggravate the burden of the debt by fresh borrowing, to live from hand to mouth, and from year to year, and to exclaim with Louis XVI: "After me, the deluge."

HOUSE OF COMMONS
*April, 1927*

*In a budget speech in the House of Commons in 1929, Churchill opposed Lloyd George's proposals to overcome unemployment by embarking on large-scale public works.*

The detailed method of spending the money has not yet been fully thought out, but we are assured on the highest authority that if only enough resource and energy is used, there will be no difficulty in getting rid of the stuff.

This is the policy which used to be stigmatized by the late Mr. Thomas Gibson Bowles as the policy of buying a biscuit early in the morning and walking around all day looking for a dog to give it to.

After Churchill's defeat in 1945, his wife, Clementine, tried to cheer him up by saying, "It may well be a blessing in disguise."

Churchill replied: "At the moment, it seems quite effectively disguised."

*Sir Stafford Cripps, one of Mr. Churchill's longtime political adversaries, was a noted vegetarian. During the postwar meat shortage in England, Churchill remarked:*

Everyone knows the distinguished talents which the right honorable gentleman [Sir Stafford Cripps] brings unstintingly to the services of his fellow countrymen. No one has made more sustained exertions to the common pot and few take less out of it than he does. I have got my vegetarian too, my honored friend, Lord Sherwell.

These ethereal beings certainly do produce a very high level and a great volume of intellectual output, with a minimum of working costs and fuel.

*In 1951, Sir Winston Churchill was returned to power after his bitter defeat in 1945. Speaking at the Lord Mayor's banquet at the Guild Hall after his triumphant victory, he said:*

This is the first occasion when I have addressed this assembly here as Prime Minister. The explanation is convincing. When I should have come here as Prime Minister, the Guild Hall was blown up and before it was repaired, I was blown out.

It would be a great reform in politics if wisdom could be made to spread as easily and as rapidly as folly.

*This conversation took place in the House of Commons in November, 1947.*

*Sir Winston:* Mr. Herbert Morrison is a master craftsman.
*Mr. Morrison:* The right honorable gentleman has promoted me.
*Sir Winston:* Craft is common both to skill and deceit.

*There was much discussion in the House of Commons over the arrangements for the Coronation of Queen Elizabeth in 1952. A Labour Party member (Mr. Glanville) suggested that contingents representing all aspects of industry and industrial life be included in the Coronation procession. Sir Winston was not overly enthusiastic about the suggestion.*

*Sir Winston:* The arrangements for the procession are in the hands of the Coronation Committee and I expect that they will recommend that only military formations should be included.
*Mr. Glanville:* Why?
*Sir Winston:* You must think of the spectators.

*Sir Stafford Cripps, Chancellor of the Exchequer, was a very diffident, standoffish man who gave the impression of always being above the crowd. It was this lack of humility that caused Mr. Churchill to remark:*

There but for the grace of God goes God.

*The heir apparent to Mr. Churchill's leadership of the
Conservative Party was Anthony Eden. Many people
wondered if Mr. Churchill was ever going to step down in
favor of Mr. Eden. Sir Winston was aware of this feeling
when he quipped:*

When I want to tease Anthony, I remind him that
Gladstone formed his last administration at the age of
eighty-four.

*The following exchange took place in the House of Com-
mons on May 28, 1952, between the then Prime Minister
Winston Churchill and Mr. Harold Davies, a member of
the opposition party:*

*Mr. Davies:* Does the right honorable gentleman realize
that the House is getting less information on the
Korean situation than his equally great predecessor,
Mr. Gladstone, was giving the House in the time of
the Crimean War?
*P. M. Churchill:* I am afraid I have not at my fingers' ends
the exact part which Mr. Gladstone took in the
Crimean War; it was even before my time.

The honorable member is never lucky in the co-
incidence of his facts with the truth.

Prime Minister Churchill was in the middle of one of his extensive surveys of the defense situation when he commented:

"I must now warn the House that I am going to make an unusual departure. I am going to make a Latin quotation. It is one which I hope will not offend the detachment of the old school tie. The quotation is *Arma virumque cano,* which for the benefit of our Winchester friends, I may translate as 'Arms and the men I sing.' That generally describes my theme."

At this point, Mr. Churchill was interrupted by Hugh Gaitskell, a Labour Party member: "Should it not be man, the singular instead of the plural?"

"Little did I expect," Mr. Churchill continued, "that I should receive assistance on a classical matter from such a quarter."

House of Commons
*March, 1953*

*Commenting in the House of Commons about the Cold War in March, 1953, Sir Winston mused:*

What we are faced with is not a violent jerk but a prolonged pull.

There is not one single social or economic principle or concept in the philosophy of the Russian Bolshevik which has not been realized, carried into action, and enshrined in immutable laws a million years ago by the white ant.

*Commenting on the British Labour Party leader and former Prime Minister, Clement Attlee, Mr. Churchill said:*

Mr. Attlee combines a limited outlook with strong qualities of resistance.

*London, April, 1951*

*Writing about Mr. Baldwin, a former British Prime Minister:*

Everybody who knew him loved him. This last must always be considered a dubious qualification.

*Commenting on the generous aid that Great Britain had received from America and the Commonwealth and the need for England to stand on her own economic feet, Mr. Churchill said:*

We have no assurance that anyone is going to keep the British lion as a pet.

BROADCAST
*December, 1951*

Our country should suggest to the mind of a potential paratrooper the back of a hedgehog rather than the paunch of a rabbit.

HOUSE OF COMMONS
*December, 1951*

The difference between our outlook [the Conserva-tives] and the Socialist outlook on life is the difference between the ladder and the queue.

We are for the ladder. Let all try their best to climb. They are for the queue. Let each wait in his place till his turn comes.

But we ask, "What happens if anyone slips out of his place in the queue?"

"Ah," say the Socialists, "our officials—and we have plenty of them—come and put him back in it, or perhaps put him lower down to teach the others."

And when they come back to us and say: "We have told you what happens when anyone slips out of the queue, but what is your answer to what happens if anyone slips off the ladder?"

Our reply is: "We shall have a good net and the finest social ambulance service in the world."

PAID POLITICAL BROADCAST
*October, 1951*


It may well be that we shall by a process of sublime irony have reached a stage in this story where safety will be the sturdy child of terror, and survival the twin brother of annihilation.

HOUSE OF COMMONS
*March 1, 1955*


Democracy is the occasional necessity of deferring to the opinions of other people.

*Addressing himself to the subject of disarmament among nations, Mr. Churchill made these rather pointed comments in October, 1928:*

Once upon a time, all the animals in the zoos decided that they would disarm, and they arranged to have a conference to arrange the matter. So the Rhinoceros said, when he opened the proceedings, that the use of teeth was barbarous and horrible and ought to be strictly prohibited by general consent. Horns, which were mainly defensive weapons, would, of course, have to be allowed.

The Buffalo, the Stag, the Porcupine, and even the little Hedgehog, all said they would vote with the Rhino. But the Lion and Tiger took a different view. They defended teeth, and even claws, which they described as honorable weapons of immortal antiquity. The Panther, the Leopard, the Puma and the whole tribe of small cats all supported the Lion and the Tiger.

Then the Bear spoke. He proposed that both teeth and horns should be banned and never used again for fighting by any animal. It would be quite enough if animals were allowed to give each other a good hug when they quarreled. No one could object to that. It was so fraternal and that would be a great step toward peace. However, all the other animals were very offended with the Bear, and the Turkey fell into a perfect panic.

The discussion got so hot and angry that all those animals began thinking so much about horns and teeth and hugging when they argued about the peaceful intentions that had brought them together, that they began to look at one another in a very nasty way.

Luckily, the keepers were able to calm them to go back quietly to their cages and they began to feel quite friendly with one another again.

*One of Winston Churchill's arch opponents in the House of Commons was the dynamic Labour Party leader Aneurin Bevan. Sir Winston's comments on Mr. Bevan frequently came in the most unexpected circumstances, as when he was speaking on the recognition of Communist China:*

As we had great interests there and also on general grounds, I thought it would be a good thing to have diplomatic representation.

But if you recognize anyone, it does not mean that you like him. We all, for instance, recognize the right honorable gentleman [Mr. Bevan].

*July, 1952*

*Toward the closing days of World War II, Aneurin Bevan pressed Prime Minister Churchill for information about the alleged installation of "reactionary governments in the liberated countries." Mr. Churchill's reply was to the point:*

I should think it hardly possible to state the opposite of the truth with more precision.

Sir William Hicks, while delivering a speech in the House of Commons, noticed Mr. Churchill shaking his head vigorously. "I see my right honorable friend shaking his head. I wish to remind him that I am only expressing my own opinion."

Churchill replied: "And I wish to remind the speaker that I am only shaking my own head."

*Once, while he was making a speech in Parliament, a member of the House of Commons became so incensed with what Churchill was saying that he jumped to his feet and tried to protest. So deep, however, were his feelings that the only sound to emerge was a gurgle. Churchill observed:*

My right honorable friend should not develop more indignation than he can contain.

Just as eels get used to skinning, politicians get used to being caricatured.

There are two main characteristics of the House of Commons which will command the approval and the support of reflective and experienced members. They will, I have no doubt, sound odd to foreign ears.

The first is that its shape should be oblong and not semicircular. Here is a very potent factor of our political life. The semicircular assembly, which appeals to political theorists, enables every individual or every group to move round the center, adopting various shades of pink according as the weather changes.

HOUSE OF COMMONS
*October, 1943*

*Speaking of Clement Attlee, the Labour Party Prime Minister, Mr. Churchill said:*

Attlee is a very modest man. And with reason.

*Mr. Aneurin Bevan was accused by the Conservatives of publishing articles abroad criticizing the British Government at a time when it was engaged in delicate negotiations. In answering these charges, Mr. Bevan first recalled that Sir Winston Churchill had had articles published in the foreign press attacking the Baldwin and Chamberlain governments, and then Mr. Bevan went on to state that Sir Winston's father, Lord Randolph Churchill, had attacked British policy in Egypt in the last century.*

*Mr. Bevan:* This criticism of his father against British policy in Egypt was uttered when there was fighting in Egypt.

*Mr. Churchill:* The right honorable gentleman has hitherto been trying to hide behind me. Now I gather he is endeavoring to hide behind my father. I am sure we can both take care of ourselves.

HOUSE OF COMMONS
*December, 1953*

*At the time of the Korean conflict, the Prime Minister was asked where all the jet planes that the North Koreans were using were coming from. The obvious answer was that the North Koreans were being supplied by the Communists. However, the Prime Minister chose to answer the question this way:*

Although there are movements ever being made in aerial locomotion, it would be premature to suppose that they came from the moon.

*May, 1952*

*During the 1922 election, Winston Churchill had an appendectomy that kept him in the hospital for all but the last two weeks of the campaign. After his defeat, he described himself as:*

Without an office, without a seat, without a party and without an appendix.

*During a discussion of international affairs in the House of Commons, a Labour Party member asked Prime Minister Churchill if, in view of the present international situation, he might reconsider taking the initiative in an effort to arrange a meeting at top level, representing the United States, the Soviet Union and Great Britain in an effort to lessen world tensions. Mr. Churchill answered:*

Perhaps on this somewhat delicate topic I may be permitted by the House to take refuge in metaphor. Many anxieties have been expressed recently at the severe character of the course of the Grand National Steeplechase, but I am sure that it could not be improved by asking the horses to try to jump two fences at the same time.

*June, 1954*

Everyone has his day and some days last longer than others.

House of Commons
*January, 1952*

The inherent vice of Capitalism is the unequal sharing of blessings; the inherent virtue of Socialism is the equal sharing of miseries.

Personally, I am in full agreement with the noble Lord on this point, and I am glad that we have found a common ground to stand on, though it be only the breadth of a comma.

HOUSE OF COMMONS<br>*July, 1910*

*Referring to Sir Stafford Cripps:*

He has all the virtues I dislike and none of the vices I admire.

*The following exchange took place in the House of Commons in June, 1954:*

Mr. *Hector Hughes (Labour Party):* Is the Prime Minister willing to reconsider his refusal to separate the Ministry of Agriculture from the Ministry of Fisheries in view of the national importance of the fishing industry and if he will now take steps to set up a separate Ministry to solve its problems and attend to its development?

*P. M. Churchill:* It would not, I feel, be a good arrangement to have a separate department for every industry of national importance. These two industries have been long associated departmentally and, after all, there are many ancient links between fish and chips.

In case, at any forthcoming general election, there may be an attempt to revive these former controversies, we are taking steps to have little booklets prepared recording the utterances, at different moments, of all the principal figures involved in those baffling times.

For my part, I consider that it will be found much better by all Parties to leave the past to history, especially as I propose to write that history myself.

HOUSE OF COMMONS
*January, 1948*

I have always noticed that whenever a radical takes to Imperialism, he catches it in a very acute form.

HOUSE OF COMMONS
*May, 1903*

*Speaking to the Canadian Parliament in January, 1952, Mr. Churchill said:*

I hope you don't mind my using the word British Empire. It is quite a good word in its proper place.

During a particularly long session in the House of Commons, one of Mr. Churchill's opponents was delivering a long-winded speech. After about a half hour, Churchill slumped into his seat and closed his eyes. The speaker noticed Mr. Churchill and said in a loud voice, "*Must* you fall asleep when I am speaking?" And without opening his eyes, Churchill replied: "No, it's purely voluntary."

When I was a schoolboy, I was not good at arithmetic but I have since heard it said that certain mathematical quantities when they pass through infinity change their signs from plus to minus—or the other way round.

This rule may have a novel application—that when the advance of destructive weapons enables everyone to kill everybody else, nobody will want to kill anyone at all.

# THE MAN

**The**

**Man**

One of Churchill's most delightful feuds was with George Bernard Shaw, who did not always approve of the Prime Minister's actions.

On one occasion, the noted playwright sent Churchill two seats to his new play and invited Churchill to attend the opening night. "And bring a friend, if you have one."

Churchill regretted that he was otherwise engaged on that evening but asked that Shaw send him two seats for the second performance, "if there is one."


Lady Astor once told Churchill: "If you were my husband, I'd poison your coffee."

Churchill replied: "If you were my wife, I'd drink it."

Mr. Churchill established a racing stable at his home at Chartwell Manor. One of his favorite racing horses was Colonist II. Once when Colonist placed fourth in a race, Mr. Churchill was ready with a reason for his horse's poor showing. He said that he had a serious talk with the horse just before the race.

"I told him this is a very big race and if you win it, you will never have to run again. You will spend the rest of your life in agreeable female company." Then Churchill added, "Colonist II did not keep his mind on the race."

*Remarking on a farm that he had just bought, Mr. Churchill mused:*

I will make it pay whatever it costs.

*Churchill loved to fly, and once quipped:*

The air is an extremely dangerous mistress. Once under the spell, most lovers are faithful to the end, which is not always old age.

*"Why do you paint only landscapes?" a friend once asked Churchill.*

Because a tree doesn't complain that I haven't done it justice.

*Jan Christian Smuts, the former South African Premier, was honored at a dinner at the White House by President Truman in November, 1946. At the dinner Premier Smuts told this story about Winston Churchill.*

During the Boer War, Churchill had come to South Africa as a newspaper correspondent and made the mistake of being captured with a detachment of British soldiers and thrown into prison. Churchill was incensed at the failure of the Boers to discriminate between a journalist and a soldier and kept shouting that he was a reporter and therefore immune to capture. But Churchill was British and seemed to be with the British Army, so the Boers couldn't tell the difference. Churchill appealed to me in a few of his well-chosen words from prison camp.

I immediately set the machinery into motion for his release but before I could accomplish this legally, Churchill had escaped from prison. Long after, I met Churchill on some state occasion and recalled the incident.

"If you hadn't been so slow," Churchill told me, "it would have cost me nine thousand pounds."

"Nine thousand pounds," I said.

"I wrote the story of my escape and sold it for that."

I have been a journalist and half my lifetime I have earned my living by selling words and, I hope, thoughts.

*Ottawa, Canada*
*January, 1952*

Short words are best and the old words when short are best of all. ´

*Churchill scribbled the following comments on a pretentious and overly detailed memorandum by one of his Ministers:*

This appears to include every cliché known to the English language except "Please adjust your dress before leaving."

Writing a book was an adventure. To begin with it was a toy, an amusement, then it became a mistress, and then a master and then a tyrant.

*London, November, 1949*

I have always been very much struck by the advantage enjoyed by people who lived in an earlier period of the world than one's own.

They had the first opportunity of saying the right thing. Over and over again, it has happened to me to think of something which I thought was worth saying, only to find that it had been already exploited and very often spoiled before I had the opportunity of saying it.

HOUSE OF COMMONS
*May, 1927*

*Churchill, on receiving notification in October, 1953, that he had been awarded the Nobel Prize for Literature:*

I notice that the first Englishman to receive the Nobel Prize was Rudyard Kipling and that another equally rewarded was Mr. Bernard Shaw. I certainly cannot attempt to compete with either of those.

I knew them quite well and my thought was much more in accord with Mr. Rudyard Kipling than with Mr. Bernard Shaw.

On the other hand, Mr. Rudyard Kipling never thought much of me, whereas Mr. Bernard Shaw often expressed himself in most flattering terms.

There is a good saying to the effect that when a new book appears one should read an old one. As an author, I would not recommend too strict an adherence to this saying.

Personally, I like short words and vulgar fractions.

*Margate, England*
*October, 1953*

*A bothersome author once asked Churchill, "Have you read my latest book?" To which Churchill replied:*

No, I only read for pleasure or profit.

Nothing in life is so exhilarating as to be shot at without result.

It is very much better, sometimes, to have a panic feeling beforehand, and then be quite calm when things happen, than to be extremely calm beforehand and go into panic when things happen.

HOUSE OF COMMONS
*May, 1935*

*During World War II, Winston Churchill often carried his own pistol, and on one occasion he took his gun out and showed it to his bodyguard, Inspector W. H. Thompson, and quipped:*

You see, Thompson, they will never take me alive. I will always get one or two before they can shoot me down.

Although always prepared for martyrdom, I preferred that it should be postponed.

When Sir Winston was asked on his seventy-fifth birthday if he had any fear of death, he replied, "I am ready to meet my Maker. Whether my Maker is prepared for the great ordeal of meeting me is another matter."

*A friend once asked Mr. Churchill if he found it difficult to sleep during the war. Churchill replied:*

Difficult? Oh no, I just put my head on the pillow, said damn everybody and went off.

*Before departing for a conference in Bermuda with President Eisenhower in 1953, Churchill turned to reporters at the airport and said:*

I will get on the plane and take my pill and I will wake up either in Bermuda or in heaven. Unless one of you gentlemen has another fate in mind for me.

*When asked by a reporter if he had any plans to retire, Sir Winston replied:*

Not until I am a great deal worse and the Empire a great deal better.

I remember it was the fashion in the army when a court-martial was being held, and the prisoner was brought in, that he should be asked if he objected to being tried by the President or to any of those officers who composed the court-martial.

On one occasion, a prisoner was so insubordinate as to answer, "I object to the whole lot of you."

HOUSE OF COMMONS
*February, 1927*

*Although Mr. Churchill is known as one of the great orators of our time, he was plagued early in life with a bad lisp. He consulted with a specialist about his lisp and said to the doctor:*

Cure the impediment in my speech, please. I'm going into the army first. But as a minister later, I can't be haunted by the idea that I must avoid every word beginning with an *s.*

*Recalling some of the darkest days of World War II, Sir Winston Churchill wrote:*

When I look back on all these worries, I remember the story of the old man who said that he had had a lot of trouble in his life . . . most of which never happened.

During my life I have often had to eat my own words and I have found them a wholesome diet.

When I survey in the light of these reflections the scene of my past life as a whole, I have no doubt that I do not wish to live it over again. Happy, vivid and full of interest as it has been, I do not seek to tread again the toilsome and dangerous path. Not even an opportunity of making a different set of mistakes and experiencing a different series of adventures and successes would lure me. How can I tell that the good fortune which has up to the present attended me with fair constancy would not be lacking at some critical moment in another chain of causation?

COLLIER'S
*April 4, 1931*

My various readings led me to ask myself questions about religion. Hitherto I had dutifully accepted everything I had been told. I had always had to go to church once a week. All this was very good. I accumulated in those years so fine a surplus in the Bank of Observance that I have been drawing confidently upon it ever since.

I have always believed in the moderate and regular use of alcohol, especially under the conditions of winter war.

When I was a young subaltern in the South African War, the water was not fit to drink. To make it palatable, we had to add whisky. By diligent effort, I learned to like it.

*Silver Spring, Maryland*
*February, 1947*

I neither want it [brandy] nor need it but I should think it pretty hazardous to interfere with the ineradicable habit of a lifetime.

All I can say is that I have taken more out of alcohol than alcohol has taken out of me.

You can't make a speech on iced water.

The human story does not always unfold like a mathematical calculation on the principle that two and two make four. Sometimes in life they make five or minus three; and sometimes the blackboard topples down in the middle of the sum and leaves the class in disorder and the pedagogue with a black eye.

What most people call bad judgment is judgment which is different from theirs at a particular moment.

I have derived continued benefit from criticism at all periods of my life, and I do not remember any time when I was short of it.

The Almighty in His infinite wisdom did not see fit to create Frenchmen in the image of Englishmen.

*December, 1942*

Free speech carries with it the evil of all foolish, unpleasant, and venomous things that are said but, on the whole, we would rather lump them than do away with them.

HOUSE OF COMMONS
*July, 1952*

I am reminded of the remark of the witty Irishman who said: "There are a terrible lot of lies going about the world, and the worst of it is, that half of them are true."

*February, 1906*

A bullet in the leg will make a brave man a coward. A blow on the head will make a wise man a fool. Indeed, I have read that a sufficiency of absinthe can make a good man a knave. The triumph of mind over matter does not seem to be quite completed yet.

At the beginning of this war, megalomania was the only form of sanity.

HOUSE OF COMMONS
*November, 1915*

It is a very fine thing to refuse an invitation, but it is a good thing to wait till you get it first.

*London, February, 1911*

The maxim "Nothing avails but perfection" may be spelled, "Paralysis."

Don't give your son money. As far as you can afford it, give him horses.

I have always considered that the substitution of the internal-combustion engine for the horse marked a very gloomy milestone in the progress of mankind.

*The following dialogue took place in Parliament on April 29, 1931.*

*Mr. Churchill:* We have all heard how Dr. Guillotine was executed by the instrument he invented.
*Mr. Samuel:* He was not!
*Mr. Churchill:* Well, he ought to have been.

Where does the family start? It starts with a young man falling in love with a girl—no superior alternative has yet been found.

HOUSE SPEECH
*November 6, 1950*

In September, 1908, I married and lived happily ever after.

It is hard, if not impossible, to snub a beautiful woman—they remain beautiful and the rebuke recoils.

# THE WAR

# The
# War

Nothing is more dangerous in wartime than to live in the temperamental atmosphere of a Gallup Poll, always feeling one's pulse and taking one's temperature.

I see it said that leaders should keep their ears to the ground. All I can say is that the British nation will find it very hard to look up to the leaders who are detected in that somewhat ungainly posture.

HOUSE OF COMMONS
*September, 1941*

*Just prior to the start of World War II, Mr. Churchill campaigned in the House of Commons for the establishment of a Minister of Supply to help meet the growing need for preparedness for possible conflict. These remarks were part of his campaign:*

A friend of mine, the other day, saw a number of persons engaged in peculiar evolutions, genuflections and gestures. He wondered whether it was some novel form of gymnastics or a new religion or whether they were a party of lunatics out for an airing.

They were a searchlight company of London Terri-
torials who were doing their exercises as well as they could
without having a searchlight.

*Churchill sent the following note to the Second Sea Lord
in 1939 at the beginning of World War II:*

Will you kindly explain to me the reasons which
debar individuals in certain branches from rising by merit
to commissioned rank? If a cook may rise, or a steward,
why not an electrical artificer or an ordnance man? If a
telegraphist may rise, why not a painter? Apparently,
there is no difficulty about painters rising in Germany.

*Commenting on the hesitant neutral nations in the early
days of World War II, Mr. Churchill made this acid
comment:*

Each one of them hopes that if he feeds the crocodile
enough, the crocodile will eat him last.

*In a speech before students at the famous Harrow School,
which was Mr. Churchill's alma mater, he said:*

Hitler, in one of his recent discourses, declared that
the fight was between those who have been through the
Adolf Hitler schools and those who have been at Eton.
Hitler has forgotten Harrow.

*December, 1940*

I stand by my original program—blood, toil, tears and sweat . . . to which I add five months later, many short-comings, mistakes and disappointments.

*October, 1940*


Russia is a riddle wrapped in a mystery inside an enigma.

BBC Broadcast
*October 1, 1939*


*Churchill was very concerned, during World War II, for the safety of the Archbishop of Canterbury, who had a makeshift bomb shelter in the crypt of Lambeth Palace. After one inspection tour of the bomb shelter, the Prime Minister turned to the Archbishop and said:*

This will never do. We must build a deeper and stronger shelter. But if, by chance, you should suffer a direct hit, I am afraid, my dear Archbishop, we will have to regard it as a divine summons.


The events in Libya are only part of the story. They are only part of the story of the decline and fall of the Italian Empire, that will not take a future Gibson so long to write as the original work.

*London, February, 1941*

*Churchill on the Blitz:*

Statisticians may amuse themselves by calculating that after making allowance for the working of the law of diminishing returns, through the same house being struck twice and three times over, it would take ten years, at the present rate, for half of the houses of London to be demolished. After that, of course, progress would be much slower.

*October, 1940*

*In reply to a question how he, who was an arch anti-Communist, could advocate support for Russia when Hitler attacked her in June, 1941, Churchill said:*

If Hitler invaded Hell, I would make at least a favorable reference to the Devil in the House of Commons.

Except for our fighting services, we have been driven back, to a large extent, from a carnivore to the herbivore. They may be quite satisfactory to the dietetic scientists, who would like to make us all live on nuts, but undoubtedly it has produced, and is producing, a very definite effect upon the energetic output of the heavy worker.

*July, 1941*

Any clever person can make plans for winning a war if he has no responsibility for carrying them out.

The intervention which I make is without precedent and the reason for that intervention is also without precedent, and the fact that the reason for my intervention is without precedent is the reason why I must ask for a precedent for my intervention.

HOUSE OF COMMONS
*November, 1941*

Most of all, I shall refrain from making any prediction upon the future. It is a month ago that I remarked upon the long silence of Herr Hitler, a remark which apparently provoked him to make a speech in which he told the German people that Moscow would fall in a few days.

That shows, as everyone I am sure will agree, how much wiser he would have been to go on keeping his mouth shut.

HOUSE OF COMMONS
*November, 1941*

When I warned the French that Britain would fight on alone whatever they did, their Generals told their Prime Minister and his divided Cabinet:

"In three weeks, England will have her neck wrung like a chicken."

Some chicken, some neck.

CANADIAN HOUSE OF COMMONS
*December, 1941*

*The Prime Minister had been criticized by some members of Parliament for the urbane fashion in which he had written to the Japanese Ambassador to inform him that Britain and Japan were at war. Mr. Churchill replied to this criticism, saying:*

After all, when you have to kill a man, it costs nothing to be polite.

When I was called upon to be Prime Minister, now nearly two years ago, there were not many applicants for the job. Since then perhaps the market has improved.

HOUSE OF COMMONS
*January, 1942*

*Prime Minister Churchill had a very ambitious Minister of Public Works. Churchill sent the following note to his minister on January 6, 1942:*

Do not let spacious plans for a new world divert your energies from saving what is left of the old.

If I am accused of this mistake, I can only say with M. Clemenceau on a celebrated occasion:
"Perhaps I have made a number of other mistakes of which you have not heard."

HOUSE OF COMMONS
*November, 1944*

*Speaking in the House of Commons about a new tank that the British had just developed, Mr. Churchill quipped:*

This tank, the A22, was ordered off the drawing board and large numbers went into production very quickly. As might be expected, it had many defects and teething troubles and when these became apparent, the tank was appropriately christened, "The Churchill."

*July, 1942*

*Charles de Gaulle was leader of the Free French in England during World War II. He proved to be a difficult man at times for Mr. Churchill to deal with. Speaking about Mr. de Gaulle after a trying meeting with him, Mr. Churchill remarked:*

We all have our crosses to bear. Mine is the Cross of Lorraine.

*At the Yalta Conference in 1945, a very tired Franklin Delano Roosevelt suggested to Winston Churchill that the conference last five or six days at most. To which Churchill replied:*

I do not see any way of realizing our hopes about a world organization in five or six days. Even the Almighty took seven.

War is a game with a good deal of chance in it, and, from the little I have seen of it, I should say that nothing in war ever goes right except by accident.

*Addressing a jubilant gathering in Paris after the liberation of France, Churchill said:*

Be on your guard! I am going to speak in French—a formidable undertaking and one which will put great demands upon your friendship for Great Britain.

*When Mr. Churchill announced in 1943 that church bells would no longer be reserved for use as a warning in case of invasion, he was asked what alternate arrangements had been made.*

Replacement does not arise. I cannot help thinking that anything like a serious invasion would be bound to leak out.

*In reply to a question at a press conference in May, 1943, when asked how a nearly defeated Italy would be treated, Mr. Churchill remarked:*

We shall continue to operate on the Italian donkey at both ends—with a carrot and with a stick.

I am sure that the mistakes of that time will not be repeated. We shall make another set of mistakes.

HOUSE OF COMMONS
*June, 1944*

When Herr Hitler escaped his bomb on July 20, he described his survival as providential. I think that from a purely military point of view, we can all agree with him, for certainly it would be most unfortunate if the Allies were to be deprived, in the closing phases of the struggle, of that form of warlike genius by which Corporal Schicklgruber has so notably contributed to our victory.

*Prime Minister Churchill had been asked by members of Parliament to rename the Minister of Defense and the Secretary of State for War on the grounds that their appellations were illogical. The Prime Minister said:*

We must beware of needless innovations, especially when guided by logic.

*December, 1942*

"Will the Prime Minister assure the House," a Conservative member asked, "that while we have quite properly attended to our physical needs of defense and of our other problems, we should not forget the spiritual resources which have inspired this country in the past and without which the noblest civilization would decay."

"I hardly think," the Prime Minister replied, "that is my exclusive responsibility."

*Matters of protocol always play a big role at diplomatic conferences. This was especially true at the Teheran Conference in 1943. A few days after the conference started, Churchill sent the following note to Roosevelt:*

I insist that I be the host at dinner tomorrow evening. I think I have one or two claims to precedence. To begin with, I come first in seniority and alphabetically. In the second place, I represent the longest established of the three governments. And, in the third place, tomorrow happens to be my birthday.

# AMERICA

## *America*


I feel greatly honored that you should have invited me to enter the United States Senate chamber and address the Representatives of both sides of Congress.

The fact that my American forebears have for so many generations played their part in the life of the United States, and that here I am, an Englishman, welcomed in your midst, makes this experience one of the most moving and thrilling in my life, which is already long and has not been entirely uneventful.

I wish indeed that my mother, whose memory I cherish across the vale of years, could have been here to see. By the way, I cannot help reflecting that if my father had been American and my mother British, instead of the other way round, I might have gotten here on my own.

In that case, this would not have been the first time you would have heard my voice. In that case, I should not have needed any invitation, but if I had it is hardly likely it would have been unanimous.

So perhaps things are better as they are. I may confess, however, that I do not feel quite like a fish out of water in a legislative assembly where English is spoken.

UNITED STATES CONGRESS
*Washington, D. C.*
*December 26, 1941*

*On a visit to the White House where he was conferring with President Roosevelt, Mr. Churchill found that he was so busy that he even had to read reports and confer with his staff while he was in the bathtub. President Roosevelt was wheeled into Churchill's quarters at the White House for a meeting and had not been told that Churchill was in the tub. As Roosevelt entered the room, Churchill was draping his wet body with a towel. The President started to apologize and was about to leave when Mr. Churchill said:*

The Prime Minister of Great Britain has nothing to conceal from the President of the United States.

The American chicken is a small bird compared with the standard English fowl. Attractively served with rice and auxiliaries of all kinds, he makes an excellent dish. Still, I am on the side of the big chicken as regularly as Providence is on that of the big battalions. Indeed it seems strange in so large a country to find such small chickens. Conscious, perhaps, of their inferiority, the inhabitants call them "squabs." What an insulting title for a capon!

COLLIER'S
*1933*

My Mother was American and my ancestors were officers in Washington's army. So I am myself an English Speaking Union.

*London, July, 1953*

We must be very careful, nowadays, I perhaps all the more, because of my American forebears, in what we say about the American Constitution.

I will, therefore, content myself with the observation that no Constitution was written in better English.

*London, May, 1953*

Nor should it be supposed as you would imagine, to read some of the left-wing newspapers, that all Americans are multimillionaires of Wall Street.

If they were all multimillionaires, that would be no reason for condemning a system which has produced such material results.

ROYAL ALBERT HALL
*London, April, 1948*

I had followed Al Smith's contest for the Presidency with keen interest and sympathy. I was in the fullest agreement with his attitude on prohibition. I even suggested to him a slogan—"All for Al and Al for All."

*New York City, October, 1947*

*Speaking to reporters at the Washington airport, after conferring with President Truman and Undersecretary of State Sumner Welles, Mr. Churchill said:*

I think "no comment" is a splendid expression. I am using it again and again. I got it from Sumner Welles.

*February, 1946*

The United States is a land of free speech; nowhere is speech freer, not even here where we sedulously cultivate it even in its most repulsive forms.

But when I see some of the accounts of conversations that I am supposed to have had with the President of the United States, I can only recall a Balfourian phrase at which I laughed many years ago, when he said that the accounts which were given bore no more relation to the actual facts than the wildest tales of the Arabian Nights do to the ordinary incidents of the domestic life in the East.

House of Commons
*September, 1944*

Winston Churchill was once asked by an overbearing American feminist about his views concerning sex equality. "What," the woman asked, "should the role of Woman be in the future?"

Mr. Churchill thought for a moment and then replied: "The same, I trust, as it has been since the days of Adam and Eve."

A dangerous, yet almost universal, habit of the American people is the drinking of immense quantities of iced water. This has become a ritual. If you go into a cafeteria or drugstore and order a cup of coffee, a tumbler of iced water is immediately set before you. The bleak beverage is provided on every possible occasion; whatever you order, the man behind the counter will supply this apparently indispensable concomitant.

COLLIER'S
*1933*

*Upon receiving an honorary degree at the University of Miami, Mr. Churchill remarked:*

I am surprised that in my later life I should have become so experienced in taking degrees, when as a schoolboy I was so bad at passing examinations.

In fact, one might almost say that no one ever passed so few examinations and received so many degrees.

From this, a superficial thinker might argue that the way to get the most degrees is to fail in the most examinations.

*February, 1946*

*Asked for his reaction to New York City, a young Mr. Churchill is said to have responded with just seven words:*

Newspaper too thick, lavatory paper too thin.

It cannot be in the interest of Russia to go on irritating the United States. There are no people in the world who are so slow to develop hostile feelings against a foreign country as the Americans, and there are no people who, once estranged, are more difficult to win back. The American eagle sits on his perch, a large, strong bird with a formidable beak and claws. There he sits motion-

less, and M. Gromyko is sent day after day to prod him
with a sharp pointed stick—now his neck, now under his
wings, now his tail feathers. All the time the eagle keeps
still. But it would be a great mistake to suppose that
nothing is going on inside the breast of the eagle.

HOUSE OF COMMONS
*June 5, 1946*

I am by no means sure that China will remain for generations in the Communist grip. The Chinese said of themselves several thousand years ago:

"China is a sea that salts all the waters that flow into it."

There is another Chinese saying about their country which dates from the fourth century:

"The tail of China is large and will not be wagged."

I like that one. The British Democracy approves the principle of movable heads and unwaggable national tails.

UNITED STATES CONGRESS
*Washington, D. C.*
*January, 1952*

92
CHU
ADLER, BILL, ed.
   The Churchill wit

| DATE DUE | | | |
|---|---|---|---|
|  |  |  |  |
|  |  |  |  |
|  |  |  |  |
|  |  |  |  |
|  |  |  |  |
|  |  |  |  |
|  |  |  |  |
|  |  |  |  |
|  |  |  |  |
|  |  |  |  |
|  |  |  |  |
| GAYLORD M-2 |  |  | PRINTED IN U.S.A. |